Black Diamonds and the Blue Brazil

Based on the book by Ron Ferguson

Adapted by Gary McNair

methuen | drama
LONDON • NEW YORK • OXFORD • NEW DELHI • SYDNEY

METHUEN DRAMA
Bloomsbury Publishing Plc, 50 Bedford Square, London, WC1B 3DP, UK
Bloomsbury Publishing Inc, 1359 Broadway, New York, NY 10018, USA
Bloomsbury Publishing Ireland, 29 Earlsfort Terrace, Dublin 2,
D02 AY28, Ireland

BLOOMSBURY, METHUEN DRAMA and the Methuen Drama logo are trademarks of Bloomsbury Publishing Plc.

Black Diamonds and the Blue Brazil by Ron Ferguson
first published in 1993 by Famedram Publishers Ltd

This stage adaptation first published in Great Britain 2026

Cover photography: Jess Shurte

Cover design: Jedly Design

A catalogue record for this book is available from the British Library.

A catalog record for this book is available from the Library of Congress.

ISBN: PB: 978-1-3506-6374-9
ePDF: 978-1-3506-6375-6
eBook: 978-1-3506-6376-3

Series: Modern Plays

Typeset by Mark Heslington Ltd, Scarborough, North Yorkshire

For product safety related questions contact
productsafety@bloomsbury.com.

To find out more about our authors and books visit
www.bloomsbury.com and sign up for our newsletters.

This production of *Black Diamonds and the Blue Brazil* premiered on 8 May 2026 at the Royal Lyceum Theatre, Edinburgh, with the following cast and creative team:

Cast

Sally	**Dawn Steele**
Dad	**Barrie Hunter**

Creative Team

Original author	Ron Ferguson
Playwright	Gary McNair
Composer and performer	Ricky Ross
Director	James Brining
Set and Costume Designer	Jessica Worrall
Sound Designer	Pippa Murphy
Lighting Designer	Simon Wilkinson
Video Designer	Lewis den Hertog
Associate Director	Jo Rush

Production Team

Production Manager	David Butterworth
Construction Manager	Jason Dailly
Carpenter/Metalworker	Sam Barker
Scenic Artist	Lisa Kellett
Painter/Decorator	Ettore Maggi
Head of Costume	Caitlin Wiedenhof
Costume Supervisor	Christine Dove
Costume Cutter	Karen Short
Costume Makers	Argyro Sapsouzidi, Grazyna Wysocka
Company Stage Manager	Dan Dixon
Deputy Stage Manager	Chariya Glasse-Davies
Technical Manager	Euan McLaren
Head of Lighting	Maria Chirca
Deputy Head of Lighting/ Programmer	Linus Pomroy

Lighting Technician/Operator	Robert Turton
Head of Sound	Ian Gibson
Sound 1	Hannah Tighe
Swing Technician/Sound 2	Morgan Yates
Head of Stage	Robin Crane
Deputy Head of Stage	John Heron
Stage Technicians	Alexandra Henderson, Chris Mundy
Apprentice Stage Technician	Ellie Tullis
Captioner	Christabel Anderson
Audio Describers	Myra Galletly, Alison Downey
BSL Interpreter	Nicolle Murdoch
Director of Producing	Callum Smith
Assistant Producer	Josephine Jay

With special thanks to Margaret Duffy and Peter Williamson for their donation and support for this production.

Cast

Dawn Steele – Sally

Theatre credits include: Suzy Kettle in *Tutti Frutti* (His Majesty's Theatre, Aberdeen); Bernadette in *Cuttin' a Rug* (Traverse Theatre); Shazza in *Rainbow Kiss* (Royal Court Theatre); Lisa Koletzky in *Verdict* (National Tour); Melissa Littleton in *Volcano* (UK tour and West End); *Skye* (Edinburgh Fringe); *Electra and Medea* (Theatre Babel); Joan in *The Perfect Murder* (UK tour); and Una in *Blackbird* (Bath Theatre Royal).

TV credits include: DCI Cora MacMillan in *Granite Harbour* (series 1–3); Stella Quinn in *Shetland*; Ange Goddard in *Holby City*; Dr Annie Jandhu in *River City*; Alice Trevanion in *Wild at Heart*; Lexie MacDonald in *Monarch of the Glen*; *Case Histories*; *Liar*; *True Dare Kiss*; *Sea of Souls*; *The Key*; *Snoddy*; *Tinsel Town*; *Haywire*; *Highlander: The Raven*; and *Split Second*.

Film credits include: *Marionette, Ghosted, None of the Above, Club Le Monde, Tabloid TV* and *Gregory's Two Girls*.

Dawn trained at the Royal Scottish Academy of Music and Drama.

Barrie Hunter – Dad

Lyceum credits: *The Breathing House, Victory, Miseryguts, The Comedy of Errors, Woyzeck, Guys and Dolls, A View from the Bridge*.

Other theatre credits include: *Small Acts of Love* (Citizens Theatre); *Blinded by the Light* (Sylvian Productions); *Grand Old Opera House Hotel* (Traverse); *The Stamping Ground* (Eden Court/Raw Material); *Smile, Tay Bridge, All My Sons, Death of a Salesman*, and *The Cheviot, the Stag, and the Black, Black Oil* (Dundee Rep).

TV and film credits include: *Scot Squad, Karen Pirie, Rab C. Nesbitt, Still Game, Dear Green Place* and *The Angels' Share*.

Barrie has worked extensively in theatre for over three decades with companies including The Lyceum, Citizens, Tron Theatre, NTS, Mull Theatre, Byre Theatre, Dundee Rep, Oran Mor PPP, Borderline, Theatre Babel and many more! He also writes/directs Perth Theatre Panto and has been the Dame there since 2011.

Creative Team

Ron Ferguson – Original Author

Ron Ferguson is an award-winning journalist, writer and minister from Cowdenbeath. He is the author of twelve books and has written for *The Herald, The Press and Journal* and *Life and Work* among other publications. He has a degree in Philosophy and History from St Andrews University, a degree in Theology from New College, a Postgrad in Theology from Duke University and an honorary Doctorate of Letters from Glasgow Caledonian University. After spending the first eight years of his ministry working in Easterhouse, Ron was Leader of the Iona Community and minister of St Magnus Cathedral on Orkney, where he still lives.

Ron wrote a biography of George Mackay Brown, *The Wound and the Gift*, which was shortlisted for a Saltire Award. His definitive biography of George MacLeod (George MacLeod: Founder of the Iona Community) was shortlisted for the prestigious McVitie's Scottish Writer of the Year Award. He also wrote a one-man play about George MacLeod, *Every Blessed Thing*, performed by Tom Fleming in London, Edinburgh, New York and Toronto. In 2017 Ron was commissioned by St Magnus International Festival to write a script for a community performance as part of Orkney's celebration of the 900th anniversary of the martyrdom of St Magnus.

Ron is a lifelong fan of Cowdenbeath Football Club, the Blue Brazil; his fifth-greatgrandmother started the club in 1881.

Gary McNair – Playwright

Lyceum credits: *Jekyll and Hyde* (with Reading Rep Theatre).

Other theatre credits include: *Dear Billy* (National Theatre of Scotland); *A Gambler's Guide to Dying, Locker Room Talk, Letters to Morrissey* (Traverse Theatre); *Nae Expectations, The*

Alchemist (The Tron); *McGonagall's Chronicles, After the Cuts, Born to Run* (Oran Mor); *Square Go, V.L.* (co-authored with Kieran Hurley) (Francesca Moody Productions); *No Regrets* (National Theatre).

Other credits include: *Tam O'Shanter, Treasure Island* (BBC Radio 4).

Awards and nominations include: Best Adaptation winner – BBC Audio Drama Awards 2025 (*Tam O'Shanter*); Winner – Scotsman Fringe First (*V.L.* 2024, *Square Go* 2018, *Letters to Morrissey* 2017, *A Gambler's Guide to Dying* 2015); Winner – Holden Street Theatre Award 2015 (*A Gambler's Guide to Dying*); Winner – BBC New Writers Popcorn Award 2024 (*V.L.*).

Gary was raised in Erskine and lives in Glasgow. His work has been translated into several languages from German to Japanese, from Italian to Arabic and performed around the world from New York to New Zealand, from Paisley to Possilpark. You can purchase many of his plays from all the usual outlets or direct from the publisher at www.bloomsbury.com.

Ricky Ross – Composer and Performer

Ricky Ross formed Deacon Blue in Glasgow in 1985, who went on to become one of Scotland's most famous and successful bands. From debut album *Raintown* and the follow-up, the chart-topping *When the World Knows Your Name*, through to 2025's *The Great Western Road*, Deacon Blue are one of the most respected and best loved bands of their generation and they continue to tour their celebrated live show around the world.

During the band's downtime Ricky has established himself as a successful solo artist and songwriter, releasing eight solo albums, his most recent 2022's critically acclaimed *Short Stories Vol. 2*, as well as writing for and with artists including James Blunt, Ronan Keating, Jamie Cullum and Nanci

Griffith, amongst many others. He has also composed music for a number of theatrical productions, at the Edinburgh Lyceum, the Dundee Rep and five major works at the Citizens Theatre including last year's re-opening production of *Small Acts of Love*.

Alongside this, he has an accomplished broadcasting career. *Another Country*, his BBC Radio Scotland show, has won two Sony awards and Ricky has twice been the proud recipient of the CMA International Country Broadcaster Award, most recently in 2024.

James Brining – Director

James was Artistic Director of Proteus Theatre Company before becoming Community Director at the Orange Tree Theatre in Richmond. In 1997, he moved to Glasgow as Artistic Director of TAG Theatre Company, later becoming Artistic Director/CEO of Dundee Rep, where he directed new and classic work including *Sweeney Todd* and *Sunshine on Leith*, winners of the UK Theatre Best Musical Award in 2010 and 2007.

He joined Leeds Playhouse as Artistic Director/CEO in 2012, directing UK tours of *Chitty Chitty Bang Bang*, *Charlie and the Chocolate Factory – The Musical* and an acclaimed in-the-round *OLIVER!* which also won a UK Theatre Best Musical Award. He directed new and classic plays including Simon Armitage's *The Bodyguard*, Arthur Miller's *The Crucible* and Zinnie Harris's *(the fall of) The Master Builder*. He commissioned 65 new plays and oversaw the £16.8 million refurbishment and rebranding of the Playhouse, which won the UK Theatre Award for Most Welcoming Theatre in 2022. His final year was among the most successful in its 54-year history.

He has also worked with opera companies across Europe, including Opera North, Welsh National Opera, La Monnaie in Brussels and Royal Danish Opera. He will direct a production of *The Magic Flute* for Malmö Opera in Spring 2027. James joined The Lyceum as Artistic Director/Joint CEO in April 2025 and has recently directed *The Seagull* in October 2025.

Jessica Worrall – Set and Costume Designer

Lyceum credits: *Girls of Slender Means*; *Group Portrait in a Summer Landscape* (with Pitlochry Festival Theatre).

Other theatre credits include: *Stand & Deliver: The Lee Jeans Sit in* (NTS/Tron); *Inexperience* (Pitlochry Festival Theatre); *The Trials* (Tron Theatre); *Small Acts of Love* (costume – Citizens Theatre); *Doubt: A Parable* (Dundee Rep); *Red Riding Hood, Comedy of Errors* (Citizens Theatre); *Henry IV Parts 1 & 2, Henry V, Two Noble Kinsmen* (Shakespeare's Globe); *After Edward, Edward II, The Treason Trial of Walter Raleigh, The Captive Queen* (Sam Wanamaker Playhouse); *Educating Rita* (Dukes Theatre); *Rites* (National Theatre Scotland); *When We Are Married, She Stoops to Conquer, Love's Labour's Lost, Wars of the Roses, School for Scandal* (Northern Broadsides); *Alice Through the Looking Glass* (Egg Theatre, Bath); *The Last Straw, Ghost Sonata, The Obituary Show, A Song without Sound?* (People Show).

Film credits include: *The Last Day, The Jossers* (dir. Gareth Brierley/People Show); *Death of a Double Act* (dir. Christine Entwisle); and *The Loss of Sexual Innocence* (dir. Mike Figgis).

Jessica also now works as a digital collage artist. You can follow her work on Instagram @jessicaworralldigitalcollage.

Pippa Murphy – Sound Designer

Lyceum credits: *Windblown* (Karine Polwart and Raw Material); *The Mountaintop, Macbeth* (An Undoing); *Truth's a Dog, Tim Crouch Wind Resistance* (Karine Polwart); *A Streetcar Named Desire, Group Portrait in a Summer Landscape* (Pitlochry Festival Theatre).

Other theatre credits include: *Enough of Him* (National Theatre of Scotland, Pitlochry Festival Theatre); *Orphans* (National Theatre of Scotland); *Total Immediate Collective Imminent Terrestrial Salvation* (Edinburgh International Festival, Royal Court, National Theatre of Scotland and Tim Crouch); *Lost at Sea* (Perth Horsecross); *Red Lion, A Streetcar Named Desire* (Rapture Theatre); *Women in Mind* (Dundee Rep); *Crude* (Grid Iron); *View from Castle Rock* (Stellar Quines/Edinburgh Book Festival); *Gilt* (7:84); *Strangers Babies* (Traverse Theatre); *Standing Wave: Delia Derbyshire* (Tron Theatre Glasgow).

Awards and nominations include Best Music and Sound Nominee – CATS (*Orphans*); Best Music and Sound Winner – CATS (*Wind Resistance*); Best Music and Sound Nominee – Broadway Baby (Lost at Sea); Scottish Album of the Year 2018, BBC Folk Album of the Year Nominee (*Pocket of Wind Resistance* with Karine Polwart).

Pippa has played piano, violin and percussion from an early age and completed her BMus, MA and PhD in instrumental and electroacoustic composition at the University of Birmingham.

Simon Wilkinson – Lighting Designer

Lyceum credits: *Group Portrait in a Summer Landscape, Castle Lennox, Christmas Tales, Glory on Earth, The Iliad, The Weir, The Lion, the Witch and the Wardrobe, Hedda Gabler, The Caucasian Chalk Circle, The BFG, Bondagers, A Christmas Carol, Cinderella, The Infamous Brothers Davenport* (with Vox Motus).

Other theatre credits include: *Sleep No More* (Punchdrunk, Seoul); *Viola's Room* (Punchdrunk, London/New York); *Bedknobs and Broomsticks* (UK/Ireland); *Islander* (US tour/off-Broadway/London/Edinburgh); *The Magic Flute* (Quebec City); *The Panopticon, Interference, The 306: Dawn, The Day I Swapped My Dad for Two Goldfish, Roman Bridge, Truant, A Sheep Called Skye* (NTS); *Dragon* (NTS/Vox Motus and

Tianjin People's Art Theatre); *What I'm Here For, Confessions of a Shinagawa Monkey, Love The Sinner, A Love Beyond, The Metamorphosis, The Dark Carnival* (Vanishing Point); *Flight, Dragon, The Not-So-Fatal Death of Grandpa Fredo, Bright Black, Slick* (Vox Motus); *Lost in Music, Our Fathers, Sex and God, Pass the Spoon, Wild Life, After Mary Rose* (Magnetic North); *Kora* (Magnetic North/Dundee Rep).

Awards and nominations include UK Theatre Award for Best Design (*Confessions of a Shinagawa Monkey*); Profile Award for Outstanding Achievement in Theatre Lighting (*Ragnarok*); Offie for Best Design (*Viola's Room*); and the CATS Award for Best Design four times.

Lewis Den Hertog – Video Designer

Lyceum credits: *One Day: The Musical* (Melting Pot); *The Mountaintop, Wild Rose* (Playful Productions); *The Outrun* (EIF).

Other theatre credits include: *Make It Happen* (Playful Productions/Dundee Rep); *When Prophecy Fails, The Afflicted* (Groupwork); *Stolen Ground* (Les Théâtres de la Ville de Luxembourg); *Escaped Alone* (Tron Theatre); *Aladdin* (Perth Theatre); *Impostor 22, all of it* (Royal Court); *Dracula: Mina's Reckoning, The Enemy, Scenes for Survival, Panopticon, Interference* (National Theatre of Scotland); *Concerned Others* (Tortoise In A Nutshell); *Daddy Issues* (White Feather Productions); *The Cherry Orchard* (The Yard and English Touring Theatre); *The Hope River Girls* (Groupwork/Imaginate); *The Wonderful Story of Henry Sugar* (Helen Milne Productions); *Wings Around Dundee, Oor Wullie, The Bridge, The Snow Queen* (Dundee Rep); *We Are In Time* (Raw Materials/Untitled Productions); *Maim* (Theatre Gu Leor); *Shaw Goes Wilde* (Pegasus Opera Company); *306: Dusk* (National Theatre of Scotland/Perth Theatre).

Lewis is a video designer and visual artist based in Glasgow, Scotland.

Jo Rush – Associate Director

Theatre credits include, as Director: *Mary, Queen of Rock!* (Edinburgh Fringe/Pretty Knickers Productions); *Ugly! A Cinderella Story* (Cumbernauld Theatre); *Stand By* (Scottish Theatre Producers); *Ivory Wings* (Edinburgh Fringe/Drayton Arms Theatre); *Design by Disaster* (Braw Fox Theatre); *Mary, The Last Farewell* (Cutting Edge Theatre Company); *Hide & Seek* (Edinburgh Fringe/Big Burns Supper Festival).

As Associate Director: *My Friend Selma* (Terra Incognita); *The Cheviot, the Stag and the Black, Black Oil* (National Theatre of Scotland/Dundee Rep Theatre/Live Theatre, Newcastle); *Heartlands* (Braw Fox Theatre).

As Assistant Director: *Death of a Salesman* (Dundee Rep Theatre); *Bloody Trams* (Traverse Theatre); *Dark Road* (The Lyceum).

Other credits include: CreateWorks Audio Dramas (Royal Academy of Engineering Ingenious Award project, Braw Fox Theatre, Edinburgh International Science Festival).

Jo trained in Drama and Theatre Arts at the University of Birmingham.

About the Lyceum

At the Royal Lyceum Theatre Edinburgh, we create outstanding theatre for Edinburgh and the world. Sitting at the heart of the city in our 140-year-old building, we welcome over 100,000 people each year. Led by our Artistic Director James Brining, we bring the best theatre from around the world to Edinburgh and share the best of Scottish theatre with the world.

We're experts in making theatre. We rehearse in our studio space across the road from the auditorium, and our costumes and sets are designed and built in house at our workshop in Roseburn, Edinburgh.

Our creative passion extends into our community and engagement efforts. In 2024, our creative learning department celebrated 25 years of developing and nurturing talent. Our Youth Theatre programmes have been the starting point for many Scottish actors, fostering newfound confidence and lifelong friendships. We also host writing groups for people aged 60+, technical courses, and training opportunities for theatre artists at different stages of their career.

Over the past 60 years the Lyceum has continued to make world class theatre – take a seat and experience it for yourself.

Writer's Note

Sport is a funny thing; when David Greig messaged me 'do you like football?' I had no idea that it would lead to me, nine years later, taking my kids to Central Park for their first ever football match, cheering on Cowdenbeath FC. But that's exactly what happened last Saturday, so there you go, that's what this club does to you.

As soon as I read Ron Ferguson's book I fell in love with the club. He has such a way of talking about the team – its history, its idiosyncrasies, its unique place in the landscape of Scottish football – that you can't help but give a bit of your heart to it. There's something deeply human that he brings out of the stories of the club and of the town, particularly across that historically poor 1992/3 season that they spent in the First Division. It speaks to the value of sport: not through success, but through losing again and again and finding the strength to keep going. Yes, as Scotland fans we all know a bit about what it is to suffer for long periods in the hope that magical, fleeting moments of success may come our way, but to understand Cowdenbeath FC is to understand something fundamental about our national psyche

It's been a pleasure and a joy to have the honour of bringing Ron's book to the stage. And to get to do that with the Lyceum is all the more special. I also feel blessed to be working with such a talented team of collaborators: Jo Rush has been an integral part of this show's life from the beginning; Ricky Ross' songs have brought such heart and soul to the show; it's a delight to see Dawn Steele, Barrie Hunter and the rest of the creative team bring their brilliance to the show; and James Brining, who has been the real Don Revie of the process – spurring all on to victory, bringing the best out in everyone.

I feel incredibly lucky and I can't wait for the show to meet an audience.

Gary

*

Thank you to:

Katy McNair
Stephen Dunn
Emily Hickman
Sally Ried
Kevin Lennon
Cora Bisset
Nicola Roy
Bruce Fummey
Phil McKee
Hannah Jarret-Scott
Pipa Murphy
Sara Mattinson
Jon Nicholls
Ciara McCafferty
Zinne Harris
Callum Smith

To all the staff at the Lyceum

A special thanks to David Greig for bringing this project, this book and this team into my life and for driving the project for so many years

The staff and supporters at Cowdenbeath Football Club for all their help over the years

And of course to the Ferguson family for their openness and generosity

For Ron,

thank you for trusting us with your words

Black Diamonds and the Blue Brazil

Characters

Sally

Dad

Narrator *is Sally when talking to the audience in direct address.*

All additional characters are brought to life by Sally.

PRE-MATCH BUILD UP

Sally OK.
So . . .
A show about Cowdenbeath?
Aye.
OK. Hold on, right.
How many of you have actually heard of Cowdenbeath?

Right and how many of you have just heard the name Cowdenbeath in passing? Like you've maybe just overheard people saying it, or heard it on like . . . a traffic report or in the classified football results and thought: what? Cowden *what*? *Beef*? What?

Right. And how many of you have actually been to Cowdenbeath?

By choice.

And of *you*, how many of you went there to see Cowdenbeath Football Club play?

Look, don't worry, this isnae dying on its arse. I wasnae expectin' many of you, well, to be honest, I wisnae actually expectin' ANY of you to have been there as they're not exactly the most supported club in the world. Well, they're no even the most supported team in West Fife, but that's . . .

Look, well, there's an obvious flaw here, right?
Surely the reason to make a show about a football team, any football team, is in the hope that partisanship and loyalty leads that team's fanbase to your show and packs it out, night after night.

So, I ask again. A show about Cowdenbeath?!

Well . . . here, for whatever reason, you are.

*

And just to be clear here, by the way
I am giving you fair warning.
I don't see you all as a group of people who are *not* Cowdenbeath fans.

No. I see you, as I see *everyone*: as a group of people who are not *yet* Cowdenbeath fans!

And if that sounds far fetched, if that sounds naive or downright ridiculous, if you're sitting there thinking;

'Sally, there's many things I could see myself becoming, but a fan of Cowdenbeath Football Club is not one of them'.

OK, sure, aye, I get it,
I do.
You've got plans, things to do, lives to live.
You may well still have hopes and dreams for the future!

But trust me, *if it can happen to me . . . it can happen to anyone.*

*

Kick Off

Right, I want to take you to Central Park Stadium in Cowdenbeath in the summer of 1992.

Song: Tonight *(Intro)*

A time before: YouTube, football podcasts and Sky Sports. A time of: fanzines and columns dedicated to lower division football in national and well-read local papers (mind those?). A time of Screamadelica, *Beverly Hills 90210* and the end of the Cold War.

Song: Tonight *(Riff)*

Anyone in the town would tell you that things are pretty special in this part of Fife right now.
Because . . . in May, *unbelievably,* this wee team, that no one's ever heard of, from this wee town, that nobody's been to's

just been promoted to the First Division for the first time in decades – there are scenes of euphoria, ecstasy, jubilation.

Song: Tonight *(Verse and Chorus 1)*

All summer, the air has sparkled with hope and anticipation as the fans dare to dream of what may lie in wait for them in their upcoming season in the big time.

And by the time that new season comes around, you will see me, right there amongst them on the terraces. Hey, I guess if ever there was a time for me to start coming to Cowdenbeath games – *this would be it, eh?*

Song: Tonight *(Verse and Chorus 2)*

Narrator And OK, right.
I know some of you might be sitting there thinking 'Oh aye, I see what's going on here – a team has a glorious promotion and you start going to the games? It sounds like *you* might be . . . a bit of a glory hunter'.

And well, to that accusation, I'll say two things;
1. No one in the history of supporting Cowdenbeath could ever, under any circumstances, be accurately described as a glory hunter
and 2.
I absolutely,
categorically,
with every fibre of my being
do not want to be here.

There is in fact nowhere on this earth, at this point in my life I'd rather be less than to be back at CentralfuckingPark in CowdenFuckinBeath.

No. Right now, in the summer of 1992, I am very much here against my will.

Song: Tonight *(Middle 8)*

Where it Really Starts

So what am I doing here?!

Well . . . you need to understand that
this story starts
with a loss.

*

It's three days earlier, I am at a funeral.

A shift, **Sally** *addresses the congregation:*

'Hello, everyone. Eh . . . Dad was a miner. As in, like he was a miner. Like, he worked in the mines, I mean. I don't mean he was a kid. Well aye, he was. Obviously. At one point. In fact at one point he was both . . . a miner *and* a *minor*. Started at thirteen! But he finished all that, long ago, to focus on his other passion – writing about football, mainly about his beloved Cowdenbeath FC. Oh, he sure did love that club. That club. His club. Your club. He really really wanted it to be my . . . oh what's the point in . . . bloody hell, I just . . . to Dad!'

Sally *is back with us:*

What a send off eh?

You'll maybe understand why I want to run and hide in a hole.
But it's not just that, it's also that, even though I am his only surviving family member, I just do not feel like I belong here.
And it's not helped by the fact that, while I am stood there dressed in black, as you would, everyone, literally everyone else, is dressed in blue and white. Must have missed that memo.

Honestly, the whole thing feels like it's more for the club than for him: there's the club flag draped over the coffin, the flowers at the foot of the catafa . . . cata . . . falque, the, the thing you put the coffin on, don't spell his name, but 'The Blue Brazil', the club's utterly baffling nickname. Even the club mascot, Bluebell the Coo is there in the front row sobbing under his unchanging wacky face. It's bordering on a fever dream.

And if I thought I couldn't feel anymore like an outsider – while I'm standing there, on my own, shaking hands, at least four people tell me . . .

'He'd be so glad you made it'.

And I tell you what . . . that stings.

Cause I know it might *sound* nice on the surface
But it just *feels* like what they're *actually* saying is:

'Oh we're surprised to see you here
given that you hardly ever made it home to see your poor old dad while he was alive. Your poor old dad wi the lungs, the bad knee and the dead wife'.

But because they don't *actually say* that,
I can't actually defend myself, can't clarify the situation,
tell them; it was, obviously, much more complicated than that
Because it *is* much more complicated than that
And then my head's swirling, thinking of the last time we spoke
On the phone
Him telling me, with so much hope in his voice /

Dad / Look Sally, I know it's a long shot, but next weekend is the last game of the season, it's away to Alloa, and if we can get a draw . . . we'll get promoted.

Think what it would mean
To me..
To the town
To see such glory.

Sally Aye, listen, Dad /

Dad / And if you could be there,
if you could join me,
aw it would just make it perfect.

Sally I'm sorry Dad, but you know I have to work Saturdays I need to /

Dad / Oh no not to worry. I understand.

Sally It's just I'm trying to be made permanent and I really need to show them that /

Dad / It's alright. As I said, I knew it'd be a long shot.

Sally . . . I'm sure you'll have a good time anyway

Dad Oh aye. Wouldnae miss it!

Narrator And I . . . I . . .

She pushes this thought down.

Sally Wouldnae have missed it!
I mean, eh, I just wish . . . *he* was here

Narrator Which prompts some arsehole to say
'He is!'
While pointing at the casket.

I make an appearance at the purvey at Wee Jimmy's Bar
But it feels even less like it's for me
It's just people singin' football songs.
So I leave and head back to Dad's.

Song: Next Time

And if I was looking for a place to feel like less of an outsider, it's not here. Cause despite living here for seventeen years, what memories come flooding back?

Dad talking about the club
But then it is quite literally just about the only thing he ever spoke about. See, when other kids
were getting magical, whimsical tales
about dragons and wizards
or tigers that would come for tea

I'd be getting:

Dad There once was a man called Ally Venters, a proper West Fife mining lad! Lads like him were proud to go straight from the pithead to the football pitch on a Saturday and play *with the coaldust still on their backs.* If you were tae cut Ally Venters in half, you'd see Cowdenbeath running through him like a stick of rock.

Ah but it's no just local lads that strut and limp through the history of this great club though, is it? We've had international talent!

Narrator The great Tewfik Abdulla anyone?

Dad Absolutely. Well he was known as Toothpick because . . . well, it sounds like Tewfik I guess, but also because he was stick thin.

Sally Aye, Dad, look, can I . . .

Dad Want a few more? Ok, well, what about the Wullies? Come on, you've got Wullie . . .

Sally Devlin?

Dad Excellent choice! Possibly the best Wullie ever to play for the club! Which is no small feat given that he himself played in a legendary side where not one, not two but . . . that's right, EIGHT of the eleven players were called William!

Narrator Great stuff, eh?

Dad OK OK, we'll do one more. We can't leave him out. A peerless genius, a legendary folk hero of unsurpassable skill. A man so unplayable that he was literally stoned by Greenock Morton fans after he terrorised their defence in a 2-0 victory to the Blue Brazil!

Narrator OK. This was a man of such mythic proportions in our house that he literally forms my first memory:

Right so I'm sat there on the carpet
and my *dad* has convinced my *grandad,* regardless of the genuine risk of severe injury that could come his way,
to demonstrate to *me*,
how the Great Hooky Leonard
used to bring down the ball and pass it
in one swooping movement.

So, stiff, puffed out, suffering from angina and about eighty-two at this point, my grandad is leaning against the fireplace so he can balance precariously on one creaking limb, while lifting the other one out to near waist height and pull down an imaginary ball and pass it gracefully out to the right wing (somewhere between the arm chair and the television set).

And all the while
Dad's sat there
splitting his enraptured focus between
his elderly father performing this treacherous feat
of geriatric athleticism,
and *me* as I take this all in as he's shouting:

Dad You see that, Sally? You see that?!

Now, we may never see his likes again, the Great James Hooky Leonard.
But this man, your grandad, actually got to see him play,
and so he lives on for us . . . through him!
And it's the stories that matter in the end, Sally!

Narrator Aye, the stories we tell ourselves, Dad.

And sure, they've gone in
But honestly, would it have killed him to have chucked the odd *Cat in the Hat* in there to mix things up a bit.

Anyway, I'm thinking: 'Right, enough "nostalgia" – I need to get to bed
so I can get up early in the morning,
get out of here
and get on with writing my *own* story'.

Song: Lullaby

Narrator But I don't get to sleep because . . .

The sound of a doorbell.

Fuck sake. What the hell could anyone want at this bloody hour?!

Well, first of all, there's this woman called Margaret
who asks if I 'want a wee sandwich. Or something'.

She has brought all, and I mean literally ALL the leftovers from the purvey. Apparently there's tuna, cheese, tuna and cheese, savoury cheese, cheese and ham. And ham. And get this:
'*Most* eh them have barely even been bitten'.

And when I . . . politely decline, on the grounds that it's eleven o'clock at night, she offers me a bowl of soup!

Sally Look, I'm sorry, but I really need to get up early in the morning so I can get back to London.

Narrator But rather than take the hint and leave, she tells me that her lad Jim '*has a Ford Montego*' who'd be more than happy to give me a lift to Edinburgh in the morning as long as he has time to '*take all of the crisps out of his boot*'.

And I really *want* to ask more but . . . then she goes on to tell me that my mother would be 'so proud of me'. And

Sally I'm sorry but I'd really rather not talk about my mum right now, thanks.

Margaret Oh. Sorry.
. . . She was such a lovely woman, she always said . . .
Sorry, it's just I . . . Sorry.
. . . And you definitely don't want a soup?

Sally No. Thank you.

Narrator So she finally leaves with her massive bag of half-eaten sandwiches.

And my head's barely hit the pillow again when

The sound of a doorbell again.

See this town! Listen Margaret, I'm sorry but I don't want any . . .

Narrator But its not Margaret, it's some friendly lookin' auld boy.

Friend of Dad's but I can't place his name.
Pat? Jim? Definitely one syllable.
Don't commit.
Just say hi.

He comes in, all timid, says

Friend How are you Sally?

Sally Well . . . I'm tired.

Narrator Then he says

Friend Shame about your dad.
Though . . . not a bad time to go, all things considered.

Sally He was fifty-three!

Friend Oh I mean more . . . timing wise. Lucky bastard!
His last game he gets to see Cowdenbeath getting promoted.
I tell you, there's no many fans round here can say they've gone out on a high.

Sally Right. Is that it?

Friend Oh, naw, sorry, just a couple things. Your dad wanted you to have these.

Narrator And he hands me a plastic bag with Dad's scarf and an envelope.

Friend That's his season ticket for this year.

Narrator And I'm like 'Fuck does he expect me to do with this?'

Takes a different tact out loud:

Sally Right well thanks for that.

Narrator But then he goes

Friend Oh, there's eh . . . one other thing, actually, Sally. I was hoping I could have, ye know . . . '*the remains*'.

Narrator And I'm like

Sally Sorry, the remains?

And he's like

Friend Aye, like . . . *his* . . . remains.

Sally Sorry, you mean, you're wantin' his . . . stuff?

Friend Naw, I mean erm his . . . *mortal* . . . remains. You know . . . his . . . ashes.

Narrator Which is . . . *sorry, hold on a fuckin'* . . . *what?*

Well . . . it turns out that Dad's made a pact with this guy that whichever of them died first, the other one would make sure that their ashes would be spread 'on the heavenly green of Central Park. After a game'.

Narrator And so *that's* how I've ended up at Central Park for the opening Cowdenbeath game of the season!

Song: Next Time *(Reprise)*

So now, rather than getting straight home and back to work, I need to stay here for three more days. Which is . . . not ideal because, well, see, right I'm a trainee solicitor, and I've landed this role at a ridiculously good law firm. It was competitive enough to get in, they only take on five or six trainees every two years but they've only ever kept maximum of two trainees on to become junior lawyers so to become one of the 'chosen few' (their words) you have to prove your dedication at all times. Everything is scrutinized. And so, time off is . . . well, aye, as I say, it's not ideal.

I phone and tell them that I '*will* actually need to discuss that compassionate leave after all' and if I'm being honest, given the circumstances, and having worked every evening and Saturday since I got there, I feel it could have been met with a little more compassion.

But it's done so I just have to accept it and prepare myself for going back to Central Park.

'Eh hawd on Sally, you just said "back to Central Park" but you clearly inferred earlier that it was your first game . . .'

Aye, very good, Rebus.
Well, OK, it's not my *first* game, but it's my first as an adult.

You see, Dad took me, well *dragged* me, to the games every week when I was wee

and he would spend all game every game feeding me information like I was cramming for an exam.

Dad See the centre half – he's a brickie.
And that winger there – he's a plumber.
The *goal keeper* . . . is a carpenter.
Now why is *that* convenient?
Because he's good with his hands!

'You know, Sally, it was the workers that built this club's rich history, and if they're to make history again, it'll be the workers that make it happen.'

Narrator And I'd nod along like I was interested but inside I was desperate for him to go get his pie so I could dangle on the hand rail for a while and dream of a bigger world than this.

So I hope, all things considered, you'd understand why I'm not exactly excited to be going back.

But look, it's one game. I can endure one game for him. Right? And I probably owe him for the eulogy.

And when match day comes I'm thinking:

Ok, Sally, you can do this.

But I'm not using his season ticket. No. I'll pay for myself, thanks.

I head out the door and

Sally *gets a big fright.*

Sally Jesus!

Narrator It's Margaret. Standing there like she's been waiting for me.
Says

Margaret *He'd be that pleased to know you'd stayed for the game.*

Sally Wouldn't have missed it.

Margaret *Here, I could walk you to the stadium, might be quite hard for you, given /*

Sally Eh . . . You're alright . . . thanks, I'll just head over myself if you don't mind. I can manage.

Narrator And I set off, ready to bring this whole story to an end.

Song: A Little Blue in the Sky *(Intro)*

Walking to the Ground

Narrator If this was a sports movie . . .
You'd see me walking to the ground.
I'd be lovingly cradling the urn under my arm, like I was encouraging Dad to take it all in, one last time. Then the camera would superimpose a sea of workers, heading en masse to the ground in their thousands, direct from the pits, to see Hooky Leonard, Ally Venters and all the Wullies playing in their pomp, you'd see the pit wheels turning in the background, but then they'd fade leaving me, a lonely figure, to carry on my journey.

If this was a sports movie, you'd see me come to a stop at the top of a street near the ground. I'd stand there frozen, staring down it. I'd lift my foot with purpose as if about to step off the precipice, then hesitate, leaving you unsure of what lay ahead and if I made the leap before we cut away.

If this was a sports movie – you'd see me enter the stadium, the camera on my face as I take it in, all of it, a look that might be awe on my face as I step through the turnstile, suggesting to you that what lies ahead is a wondrous landscape.

Song: A Little Blue in the Sky *(Part 1)*

But this is *not* a sports movie,
so in reality I held Dad out at arm's length the whole way here, terrified that I might . . . spill him. And I did not stop at the top of that street for a second. I ran right past it without even looking down it. I made a deal with myself a long time ago that I would never walk down that road again, and I wasn't going to go back on that today. Opting instead to go the long way round to the stadium.
And as for the look on my face – well, while it might be true, there certainly is no football ground quite like it; between the rundown coconut shies and waltzers, the stock car racing track that is literally going right around the pitch and the sign overhead that reads 'Spectators Enter at Own Risk' it feels a lot less 'theatre of dreams' and a lot more 'if Ken Loach made *Blade Runner*'. So what might have read as 'awe' would much more likely be 'aw . . . naw'.

Anyway, I find Tam, Tom – Tim? Whatever, don't commit – and his friends.
They're all laughing and apologising to my dad in the urn as they discover that he was telling them the truth that he did in fact call me Sally 'Venters' McAlpine after, yes, his all-time favourite Cowdenbeath player – Ally Venters.

Narrator The chat turns to today's game and, despite the recent glory of promotion, the guys are all in complete agreement that they're *almost certain to 'get pumped' today.*

Well, let's get this over with . . .

Sally Come on TEAM!

Narrator And the game is . . . well, it's boggin, rotten, howfin. Absolutely brutal viewing, my god, but that's alright, because it's done.

Pat, Geoff, Cole, whatever, says:

Friend That was great! I know it was a draw. But it really '*felt like a win*'.

Narrator Which I don't really understand, but then he says that Dad 'would have loved it' and well, aye, I have to agree with that. I'm pretty sure he would have.

She holds the urn, takes a beat.

So I steady myself and . . .
'Well Dad, you did it, you got me to a match. Well done. Right. You ready?'

I slowly make my way out to the centre circle.

But then *he* says 'Sally, what you doing?'
And I'm like 'I'm . . . gonna spread Dad's ashes . . .'
And then he gives me this look,
and says '*Oh . . . did I not say? Your dad's wish was actually . . . for his ashes be spread out on the centre spot of Central Park . . .*

after . . .

a win'.

Sally Eh . . . no. No you . . . did *not* say that.

Song: A Little Blue In The Sky (*Verse*)

Back at the House

Sally 'Hi, so, look I'm sorry but I am going to have to extend my compassionate leave. I know, I know, I'm sorry, but there's just something I need to . . . yes, no, you're absolutely right, no I don't want all my hard work to go to waste, no. Yes, I do understand. Yes, I *am* committed to the team. But. Well, that *does* sound like a very generous offer from Douglas, but I don't need him take some of my work load till I'm back (sneaky bastard). Trust me I'm on top of it . . . Yes, I know grief can . . . affect performance, but, look, you can rely on me, just three more days, then I'll be back and I can, yes, OK, ye'.

Narrator So, a win? And four more days here? How hard can that be?

And look, it's not that I hate the place, I really don't, it's just I hate . . . being here.

Dad Sally, I know London's exciting and that but where's the need? Anything London's got, you can get here.

Sally Oh aye, I'll just pop out for a nice coffee on my way to the Cowdenbeath Portrait Gallery shall I?

Dad Well, ah've a jar eh Maxwell House in the cupboard. And we've an exhibition at the social club of all the players that died in World War Two. It's moving stuff. And some very striking portrait work.

And hey, look, it was good enough for royalty, eh?
Queen Victoria liked to stay at the Station Inn here!
And Mary Queen of Scots, she loved it so much that, when she passed through, she was said to have asked her coachman, *Quels beaux Champs de Fleur*?
That's how they got the name 'Jamphlars' – which, aye, is a piece of linguistic reductionism that, shall we say, fails to capture the romance of the original. But it's a good place. And /

Sally Look, Dad, I know. I just . . .

Dad OK, OK, right, what do Sir James Black, the Nobel Prize-winning inventor of the beta blocker, Professor Duncan Reekie, chairman of Economics at Johannesburg Uni / versity,

Sally / Dad

Dad Professor Agnes Jarvie, Professor Richard Scott

Sally Dad

Dad Professor Gillies, Belfast /

Sally / Dad, they all went to Beath High School

Dad Aye. And what about Professor Philip, Chair of Infectious Diseases / and Immunology at Bowman Gray School of Medicine, North Carolina

Sally / Beath High School.

Dad What about bestselling novelist Ian Rankin, Covent Garden opera star Elaine Hall, Stuart Adamson of the Skids and Big Country, principal clarinetist / for Scottish Opera Lewis Morrison

Sally / They went to Beath High School!

Dad What about celebrated Rangers and Scotland star Jim Baxter? (He should have played for us by the way!)

Sally I get it, they were all educated at that international seat of higher learning, Beath High School, Cowdenbeath.

Dad OK, but what about former Minister of the Arts, founder of the Open University, Baroness Lee of Asheridge – aka Jennie Lee? One of the greatest Scots of the century, a firebrand in turbulent times, the very reason you want to study law! Honed her political rhetoric on these very streets with its pit disasters, gritty humour and radical politics in its DNA.

Sally Aye, Dad, she made all that to make a difference in the world, I want to do that too. But crucially, in order for her to do that, she, like all the others you've mentioned, left here to do it.

Dad Aye, but . . . doesn'y mean it was necessarily right. Jim Baxter, he said he wished he'd played for us, regretted never doing it, and if you think that's frustratin' for us to hear, how do you think he felt? Knowing he could have given his brilliance to the people of the town that made him? Look, I know you want to do good in the world, and I'm sure you will, but . . . just, like, maybe this place needs some great people to, you know, do good here . . .

Sally Look I'm no even sayin' I'm goin', I just . . . I don't know . . . Maybe . . . one day.

Dad Aye, maybe one day.

Narrator So, four very slow and painful days pass, match day arrives, I carefully pop dad in my bag
and I head out.

She heads outside.

Sally AH! Christ.

Narrator Margaret again.
Offering, again, several times this time, to walk me to the game.
I tell her, *once again*, that

Sally I can manage. Thanks.

Narrator I get to the ground. The long way. And . . . when I see the crowd, largely due to the travelling support, is *so much bigger* than the last game. And when I hear the abuse they're shouting: everyone's calling each other all sorts and Bluebell the Coo's holding his nose next to the away fans, suggesting they stink, I realise who they're playing today.

Then John, Paul, George? Whatever's like:

Friend This is more like it, eh Sally? This is a better game for your dad to go out on.

Narrator And well, aye. You see, Dad lived by a golden rule:

Dad Sally. You should be kind to everyone you meet. I truly believe that.

And I believe that treating everyone as a true equal is your only shot of finding peace and happiness.
However.
I am a realist.
And therefore I believe you also need a release.
A valve. A means by which you can
let all your negative feelings out so that you can maintain peace and harmony in the rest of your life.
So, what I do is, I reserve all my hate and frustration and anger and I direct it exclusively towards . . . Dunfermline.
It may not be perfect. It may not be ideal.
But I tell you, it's effective.

Narrator *So, aye,* if he needs a win, there's no team he'd rather beat. So, here's hoping they can do it for him today . . . against Dunfermline.

Song: One of these Days (Let's All Laugh about Them)

Narrator And . . . well, the more perceptive among you out there have probably already guessed that, what wi given how long there probably is left of the show and all that, that, well . . . naw . . . they *didnae* do it for him today against Dunfermline.

Song: One of these Days (Let's All Laugh about Them)

Sally I HOPE YER NEXT SHITE'S A HEDGEHOG!!!

Song: One of these Days (Let's All Laugh about Them)
(Middle 8 Reprise)

Sally But . . . they . . . they were . . . so bad . . .?

Narrator And Sam, or . . . Bill or whatever's like

Friend Well aye, we're Cowdenbeath.

Sally Aye, but . . . What about the 'jubilation and euphoria' I kept hearing about in the summer? What about the 'genuinely brilliant team that captured the hearts and minds of the nation' and got promoted?

Friend Oh, well they're, eh . . . all gone

Sally Sorry, whit . . . '*gone*'?

Friend Well, eh, most eh them, aye.
You see . . . rather than build on the success of promotion by signing a few better, more experienced players in key positions, *the board* decided to have a wee civil war and hand out more P45s than the Wimpy oot in Kircaldy after the Great Food Fight of '87, which sees them get rid of *most* of their promotion players *and* sack the manager, John Brownlie, that lead them there, in the process!
And they've brought in some new manager that has not only never managed a professional team in his puff but he's had to scramble around for the last few weeks to find any players he can to make the numbers up. Which is, all respect due, about the most Cowdenbeath thing Cowdenbeath could do.

Narrator So as the ground's emptyin' around us I'm thinking . . .
'Fuck this! This is madness. I know this club's history, unfortunately, I know how rare a good Cowdenbeath side is! I cannae wait around for this new team to win a game, I've got a life to live. Well . . . I'm busy. I've not worked all these hours to chuck it away to come back and watch this shower of shite again. I'm Six Day Sally, I'm Sally Saturdays, I've worked too hard. Given up too much, and now I've got Slippery Douglas circling to take all my credit.
Look I know it's not what he wanted, and I'm sorry, right, but . . . I tried'.

And even though it feels wrong,
I'm just about to *do* it
When I hear /

Friend / Listen, Sally, don't worry pal,
he'd understand if you . . . can't make it to the next game.
It'll be alright,
we'll make sure that it happens for him.

Narrator And I know he's just trying to be nice. And I know I had just decided, ten seconds ago, that I was gonna spread his ashes right now, against his will, after a *defeat* to his *worst enemy*, go back home to London and never return. Still, him *suggesting* that that *might* be the case, I . . . I . . .

Sally Of course I'll be there!

Narrator And he says

Friend Aw that's wonderful, Sally. It really is.

Sally Aye, it's just perfect.

Narrator So, I finally get back to work where I try to rebuild my reputation as a 'driven and committed member of the team' after the whole 'taking compassion leave' drama, but I know that in two-and-a-half weeks I'm going to have to find a way to get back there. And I can't risk asking for the Friday off to travel up for a game, not being in on the Saturday is bad enough, they're not contracted but are an 'expected extra' of potential chosen ones. So I work as late and as long as I can while I'm back, even adding Sundays, hoping that's enough for them not to mind that I'm leaving at 9.15 p.m. on a Friday to head for the night bus, hopin' it's third time lucky for a win.

And the night bus is . . . well I've got a guy beside me drinking what I'm sure is a bottle of vinegar and someone somewhere is singing 'Moon River' all. Night. Long. So . . . the night bus is . . . the night bus. But it's needs must. Get up the road. Get the win. Get home.
There's no chance I'm getting any sleep, or any work done. And I've got Dad goin' round my head, giving it:

Dad Sally, you're young and full of hope. And that's great. Commendable. But before you get fanciful notions in your head from things you might have seen about football in the movies, you have to understand that 'winning' is not something that we do very often.

Sally Great!

Dad Don't get me wrong, we have won things, just . . . no very much.

We won the second division title in the 23/24 season

Narrator (That's the 1923/24, season just to be clear.)

Dad But that's not all, no – we've won something truly special – Scottish Premier League? The European Cup? The B&Q Paints Challenge Trophy? No, this is something no other club in the world can lay claim to – that's right, we once won *nine* fish suppers off a cocky wee toff of a goalkeeper from St Andrews University that bet that Cowdenbeath wouldnae put more than three goals past him.

How's about that?!

But look, the point is, I'm telling you – it really isny all about winning.

Narrator Aye, except, now, thanks to him . . . it is!

The bus sputters into Edinburgh at seven,
grab a quick sleep and a pit wash at Dad's,
deal with Margaret
and head to the ground, the long way round, hoping I never have to do this again.

But erm . . .

We watch **Sally** *watch the game.*
It does not go well.
They are pumped 5-1.
We can see the horror on **Sally**'*s face.*

*

So, September 4th . . . after another fortnight of working every hour under the sun, I'm on another Friday night bus.

Again, no sleep. Again, more Dad:

Dad Sally, you know what's important? Struggle! It is! It's the struggle that sets us up to endure injustice and hard times. It's a sad fact of life, Sally, that everyone, unfortunately, dies.

However . . . there is something that never dies . . .

Sally Love?

Dad Cowdenbeath Football Club!

Oh we've come close. Many times!

We've had more emergency general meetings to decide on whether or not the club should fold due to massive debts than we've won fish suppers (and as you know – we won nine of those).

Look, the fortunes of the club would always rise and fall with the fortunes of King Coal.

But somehow, we've always found a way – an injection of cash from a local business, a fund raising drive from the fans . . . Cup wins! They're great. Good money in that. Can keep clubs like us alive.

I mean, it'll no buy you George Best, but it might pay to get a guy out to try and stop the bees from flying over the wall into the back of the main stand from April til' September.

But, look, they always find a way. The stock car racing track – that's been a real life saver for the club for years.

You know, it was actually originally built as a greyhound track, the same year Wullie Curle (another great Wullie, by the way) scored six goals against Hearts of Beath and was rewarded with six pounds of sausage from a local butcher but that's neither here nor there.

The point is . . . there's nothing wrong wi a bit of struggle. It's good for ye.

Narrator *I mean, even just statistically at this point, you'd think it has to be coming.*

Well if it's coming. It's no coming today!

The score flashes up: 1-0 to Dumbarton.

Another fortnight later. Another night bus.

On the bus.

Dad Sally, I'm tellin' you, it's no all about the winning!

Let me remind you – I was there.

September 1949, Central Park. I'm ten years old.

With over 25,000 other people, more than twice the population of the town, to see if we could be the first Second Division side in history to dump the famous Glasgow Rangers out of the League Cup.

And we nearly did!

I know because I was there.

On the verge of the most famous victory in Scottish football history.

With thirteen seconds to go.

We have the ball up the Rangers end.

Big Ming shouting:

'Don't try anything clever, Frank. Just boot it down number seven pit!'

But then . . .

I can still see it in slow motion.

I'm weepin'. My father's weepin'.

Big, hard miners are weepin'.

Sure, we lost that day, but we got to taste something greater than victory, something most other teams would never understand. We felt, for a very real moment, hope. We had genuine belief that we could achieve greatness. Did I tell you, I was there? I'll never forget it.

I'm telling you Sally, some things are more important than winning.

Narrator Oh thanks Dad, I'll keep that in mind if they happen to 'get pumped' again today.

When I get there Auld One Syllable seems . . . chipper, giving it:

Friend Did you hear Sally? Did you hear?
We went to Somerset Park last Saturday to play Ayr United . . . and we won!!
Isn't that brilliant?

Narrator But all I can think is

Sally First of all, it was away from home, so what use is that to me?
And secondly . . . well I may as well just go back to London now because there is absolutely no way this team are winning two games in a row!

Friend Ach come on Sally, you never know!

Narrator Well, is this when they turn a corner?
Is this is the moment it all clicks?
Is this the moment I've been waiting for, when they bless us with a home win?

The sound of the anticipation of a crowd builds, then crumbles.

No.

Ted, Rod, Ged philosophises that:

Friend You know what? I think we might be in for a long season.

Narrator And eh . . . well . . .

'Don't I know it'.

*

Narrator And when I get to the next game, Auld One Syllable is as desperate as me. He says:

Friend . . . Think we might need a bit of help

Narrator And he clasps his hands in prayer!

Now, I can't help point out the flaw in his plan – that 'unless the big man is a Cowdenbeath fan, and I think we can all agree that there is some serious evidence to suggest that he *isn't*, I don't think it will bring us much luck.'

To which he says:

Friend Well, what harm can it do?

Narrator And he asks the divine hand if he could 'see to it that we score one more than them'.
And would you believe it . . . it works! Because with six minutes to go of a very tight game, Eric Archibald of Cowdenbeath rises high above all the St Mirren players and scores an *absolute peach* of a header!

Into his own net.

This bloody team!

Sally Can this season get any worse?!

Narrator Well, it turns out it *can* because . . .

Music: One Of These Days *(Instrumental Reprise)*

Narrator . . . One, we're now in October. And two, while the next game in two weeks is on a Saturday, if they don't win *that* I'm in real trouble because the next game after *that*'s just four days later. On a Wednesday. A bloody Wednesday. There's no amount of extra hours you can work to get around that. That's a whole different ball game, that's applying for a day off, HR, forms, written record of time off, it's pretty much handing in my resignation.
So . . . I decide to pull a sickie. But I'm smart with it, spend a few days getting increasingly sick, to both lay the groundwork for it while hopefully earning some credit for

having fought on like a trooper for as long as I could. But as I'm leaving on Friday night, I'm pulled into the boss' office and he says 'I get it Sally, I do, I love Scotland, I have a little place there, I feel its pull, it's richt bonnie, it is, but that pull is clearly affecting your work. And now your health. So I've decided to give some of your workload to Douglas, just til you sort yourself out and ask yourself if you're really, you know, on the team'.

I pass Douglas' desk on the way out, see his little name plaque that just says 'winner' on it and I want to bludgeon him with it but I figure I'd miss the bus cleaning up the blood. So I just keep walking.

And then, to make things worse, when I get back to dad's, wondering if it wasn'y actually *me* that's died and that this isn't actually just some sort of purgatory, the door goes.

And it's

John John McWhirter. From the council.

Narrator He's wanting the house back.

I explain the . . . situation and he says

John Well, while that's all very compelling and all . . . this is not a hotel, Miss McAlpine.

Sally . . .

John There is a process. As the next of kin, if you want to live here, you have to apply to do so with the council. I can give you three months.

Sally Listen, I don't *want* to live *here*. I know it might *look* like I want to live here. But it's only until Cowdenbeath win a home game!

John . . . You have to understand there is a waiting list, Miss McAlpine.

She changes tact.

Sally Do you know what, actually, John McWhirter, from the council. I'm a lawyer. Well . . . I *have* a law degree.
And I'm *pretty sure* I've got rights here.
Now, I don't know exactly what those rights are,
but I'm . . . pretty sure I have them. Alright?!

Narrator Then he hands me a card, should I wish to discuss those rights with him.
The card tells me his office . . . is in Dunfermline.

*

Narrator *So, I now appear to be squatting*
in my dead dad's house where I don't want to be staying, in a town I don't want to be in,
so I can go to football games I don't want to watch!
While the life I'm building for myself is going to fuck!

Dad Sally, we're lucky, you and I.

Sally YOU SURE ABOUT THAT?!

Dad Well, it's no been easy.

Look. The whole time I worked down the pits, I did it with the memory of disasters like the Mossmorran collapse in my mind, we aw did, knowing that at any point we could be seconds from catastrophe. We all knew the true cost of they black diamonds was ultimately paid in blood and that true solidarity meant walking into what could be certain death, to join the search for your fellow miner if needs be.

So when the Lindsay Pit disaster happened, in we went.

But David Scott, who I worked beside for years, and stood beside on they terraces, never made it back out.

Nine others died too.

And why? Well, they said it was because someone had lit a cigarette and bang and the place went up.

Dying for a fag, eh.

Point is, Sally, sometimes horrible things happen.

And it's not just in the mines.

Needless, random, terrible things happen all the time.

When I was eight, we turned up at school to our teacher telling us that wee Andrew Cree had been taken by the angels to Jesus. That's all we got. And we just had to try and play and learn while his chair sat there empty.

David Scott, Andrew Cree and all the other names live on while we're left trying to make sense of it.

We are lucky Sally. It might not feel it but we are.

Narrator Aye well . . . you know what, I don't feel very fuckin' lucky, actually, I feel like you've trapped me in some guilt trip punishment from beyond the grave to make me suffer as much as you did! I feel . . . pretty pissed off actually, dad. In fact, I'm raging.

When I get to the game I am screaming at them to win. To just win one fucking game and get this whole thing over with so I can get back to work tomorrow and try to salvage what's left of a career I've worked my arse off to build and that this team has tried so hard to destroy.

Does it work?

. . .

. . . Does it fuck!

And to make matters worse, when Willie Callahan scores a last-minute goal to snatch a draw for Cowdenbeath,
the crowd goes wild.

And I. Am. Ragin'.

Sally Are you guys for real? Is this really what passes for excitement these days?!

Narrator And they're all like.

'Oh come on, we need to enjoy moments like these when they come!
That was incredible.
Those Stirling Albion boys'll think twice before they come here again!'

Sally Listen to yourself!
This isn't good.
It might be as good as it *gets* but that doesn't make it good!
How can you be happy?!

Friend Sally, there's nothing *wrong* wi . . . being happy.
Come on, lets go to the pub. My round!

THE BLUE BRAZIL! THE BLUE BRAZIL! THE BLUE BRAZIL!

Sally Look at the state of you!
Celebrating this '*like it's a win*'?
But it's not a win.
It's a fucking draw!
Which means for me – it's a loss.
Another loss!
And I'm tired of losing.
Lost my dad.
Losing my job.
I can't lose any more!
It *needs* to *be* a WIN!
But of course I need it from this team that has literally *never* won *anything* in its life apart from nine fuckin fish suppers!

What the fuck is wrong wi you people?!!

Sally *leaves. Irate.*

Song: What We're Doing Here

HALF TIME

SECOND HALF

Song: Jamphlars

A Memory

Sally *sits, cross-legged, looking at her dad.*

Dad Sally, there's something that, as your father, I think it's only right to tell you. It's something you need to know as it will likely affect *you* later in life too.

Sally What is it, Dad?

Dad I'm sick.

Sally What?! You're what?!

Dad Unfortunately I suffer from a rare and, I'm so sorry to say, hereditary disorder that has no known antidote. Once it attacks the brain, it shuts down the cells responsible for rational thinking. For good.

And there's no brain surgery, or analysis, no cognitive therapy – or even electric shock treatment available that can cure this rare and compulsive disorder.

Sally Dad, what's going on?

Dad All I know is that my father had it, my grandfather had it and now I have it.

Sally Have what dad? Tell me!

Dad Sally, I'm afraid I suffer from what's known as Mad Cowdenbeath Disease.

Sally Dad!

Dad Well it's true! Why else would I find myself waiting all week long, while the will to live ebbs away, to pitch up on a litter strewn, Kafka-esque stadium in Cowdenbeath to participate in a West Fife Tourettes convention and watch a brand of Scottish football which mostly feels like a rehearsal for purgatory?!

Sally You could just stop.

Dad Sometimes I wish I could, but the things is . . . I can't.

I think it might be the stories – they're formative. They lay down the neural pathways in the brain. They shape who you are. They provide the mental and spiritual lenses through which we see the world. I was brought up in the faith – indoctrinated some would say.

Sally Tell me about it.

Dad Look, whatever the cause, one thing's for sure – Mad Cowdenbeath Disease is incurable. And once it takes hold, Sally, there's nothing you can do about it.

Sally Well I certainly don't have it.

*

Back to Reality

Narrator This other formative memory is served to me as I somehow find myself on yet another night bus from London in order to stand in that very litter strewn, Kafka-esque stadium.

Ah but Sally, what happened to the Wednesday game, the one you had to pull a sicky for after your wee meltdown? Well, I'm glad you asked – it was against lower division Montrose in the B&Q cup, a match I was told was 'almost certainly guaranteed to be a win' . . .

Sally HA!

The score flashes up.
Cowdenbeath 0-4 Montrose

Narrator And seeing as the next game was at Halloween Why don't I tell you how that went in the form of a joke:

Knock knock, who's there? It's Greenock Morton, with a comprehensive 3-1 gubbing.

Narrator Which brings us to, that's right . . . November. November?! (Mind how I just needed a win. A single win. In August!)

But not to worry, this next game is against Hamilton, who are the only team in the league we haven't played at home this season. And well

Friend If you think about it Sally, we've got *to beat somebody . . . right?!'*

Cowdenbeath 0-3 Hamilton Academical flashes up.

Sally Do we, aye?

Friend *Well, at least we get to play everyone again.*

Sally *Well, that's just . . . fuckin . . . superb!*

Song: Andrew Cree

*

The December Games

Narrator So it's December. And while everyone else at work is spending their Friday and Saturday nights on Christmas nights out, networking and proving what good team players they are, where am I?

Sally NOT TODAY MARGARET!

Narrator OKk, so how about some Christmas cheer then: right . . .

(*Chants.*) *In the first game at Christmas,*
Cowden took the lead
And they scored again
But Kilmarnock
They scored three.

In the second game at Christmas
Cowden took the lead
And they scored again
But so did Ayr United
Who then equalised
And a draw's no use to me.

In the third game at Christmas
Cowden took the lead
But they weren't playing good
The small crowd booed
And be-fore our eyes
To no-one's surprise
We watched as Clydebank scored three.

Fuckinbastardlousystupidnogoodfuckintwobitpieceoffucki-naaaaaargh

Friend I guess I'll . . . see you in the new year then, Sally?

Narrator I gather myself and, hearing that, that this is now stretching into a second calendar year, I just . . . I nod and say '*wouldnae miss it!*' but inside I'm thinking – man, I . . . don't think I can . . .

Song: Andrew Cree *(Reprise)*

*

Narrator At this point, there's actually a month until the next home game, which gives me a chance to put them out my head for a while and throw myself into my work. And I go hard at it. Move over Sally Saturdays, Sally Sundays is here. I'm working seven days a week to really show them who I am. And show Douglas who he's up against. I work Christmas Day, Hogmanay, New Year's Day too. Why not?! And I tell you what, it's working. Boss comes to me, says, 'Bravo Sally, there's the coal miner's attitude we've come to expect from you. It's good to have you back'.

Ye see? See what happens when I get a month away from that place?

And this is it, this is the time. They're picking their 'chosen few' any day now, so that's it – if I've somehow clawed back a shot at glory from that place's shitey jaws, I can't throw it away now by going back! And OK, that means I won't be there when they do eventually win . . . and aye, it means Bob or Jim or Dan'll have to spread Dad's ashes on his own but . . . look, naw, I tried. But I'm done. Have to be. New year. New me.

And you know what? I don't even think about them once. OK, I check the scores.

Not because I care. Because I don't. I just . . . I . . .

OhIdon'tknowitdoesn'ymatterI'mnogoin'back!

I'm moving on.

And about a fortnight into 'new me', Boss comes in and tells me 'Sally, word on the street is you are IN! Nothing set in stone yet, but, there's a big gala dinner on Saturday with the partners and if you make a good impression there, show your commitment to the team, and it's as good as done. Providing of course you don't, as my father would say to my mother when she'd iron his Pierre Cardin suit, find some way to fuck it up. So, what do you think?'

Sally Oh, I wouldny mi . . . eh, I mean, absolutely. Thank you.

Narrator Fuckin' yassssss.

Not Going

Narrator You see? It was that place. I knew it!
And now the Friday night before that next home match has finally rolled and where am I?

Am I on a nightbus to Cowdenbeath so I can see them play Meadowbank Thistle?

No. I am skipping home because, after attending thirteen home games in a row, I have set myself free!

I can do anything I want tonight!
I could go to the pub.
I could go to a gallery opening.
A West End show!
Could go and see what this *Phantom of the Opera* is all about.

Dad Did you know that James Patterson, one of the original cast members of *Phantom of the Opera*, was from Beath High School?!

Narrator Ach . . . well maybe *Les Mis* then!

But anyway I've got no friends to go to the pub with, I don't know how you go to a gallery opening,
and I cannae afford to go to a West End show,
but that's not the point.
The point is I *could*. Theoretically. Do anything.
Because I am in *control* of *my own* destiny.

So I do the next best thing, I have a bath and watch *Heartbeat*.

Then I drift effortlessly off to sleep because tomorrow I get to show the world that I am Sally McAlpine. And I am a winner!

But then it's 3 a.m.
and suddenly I wake up in a shaken panic.

AH! *Fuck*. What if they win and I'm not there and I've missed my chance to be actually, properly free from this?!
No. Sally, you've been over this. You're just tired, get back to sleep and it'll all feel fine in the morning.

But I don't get back to sleep and it doesn't feel better in the morning, cause it's half eight and I'm thinking: Right, *if I went for a train right now, I could probably still make it to Fife for kick off.*

Come on Sally, listen to yourself!
Nine o'clock. I'm making breakfast. *Don't do it Sally.*

9.30. I'm grinding my coffee and I'm looking at the tube map!
Now stop it Sally! This is ridiculous. It's just that place trying to . . .
No. Stay strong.

9.45. I'm on the sofa. Coffee in hand. Feet are up.
I am *here. I am going to the gala later, I am going to impress, I am going to fit in, I am going to get what I deserve.*

In the meantime.

I'm gonna to relax. I'm gonna . . . read a book. I'm gonna . . . I'm gonna . . . I'm gonna . . . fuck I'm gonna go, amn't I?

No. Do not get off this sofa. You are going nowhere. You. Are. Going to. Relax.

Look at me.
Look at how relaxed I am.
Right?!

Tell you who's *not* relaxed? Anyone who's getting ready to go see that lot.
Torturing themselves, thinkin:
'*Oh, maybe. Just maybe. Today will be different*'.

'Maybe today'll be different?' HA!
State eh them! Aye, maybe it will.

Aw fuck, maybe it will?! Maybe today *WILL* be different!

Oh . . . bloody hell!

It's ten o'clock.
Coffee's hit my system, folded right into the anxiety and shame, any hope of relaxation is shot to fuck and I'm grabbing my bag.

Sally, this is not happening. Turn around, right now! This is the behaviour of an unhinged person.

At the very least its the behaviour of a person whose entire future is not depending on them needing to be in London, tonight!

How? How are you managing to make the agony of going to a Cowdenbeath game even more agonising! Just turn around now and /

/ 10.26, I'm at the station and ah fuck. There is. There's a 10.30 to Edinburgh and /

Sally, you need to stop this madness while you still can. There's no way you are getting on that train. Do not get on that /

/ It's 10.31 and I'm pulling out of King's Cross station

And at some point on that journey,
I realise

Oh God, it's happened.
I've contracted Mad Cowdenbeath Disease.

So. Change trains at Waverley. Pull into Cowdenbeath station with about fifteen minutes of the match to go and get to the stadium five minutes later and

I can't believe it!
I look at the scoreboard and

Sally (*pointing at the board*)
My god, is that a joke?

(*Delighted, but another thought . . .*)

Is it . . . a mistake?

My god, they're winning!

See?! See when you follow your gut and you take a risk!

I knew it. I just knew!
I could feel it in my bones. In my heart. I knew.

Work'll understand. They have to. Cause like, it's over now.
Now I'm actually free!

I look around at the punters' faces.
Faces that have looked so miserable all year, are now a blend of joy and disbelief.
And it's not about winning, eh Dad?

To think I nearly missed this.
Missed this atmosphere.
Missed this relief.

Nearly missed the passion. The determination. The fight to cling on.
Nearly missed the big centre half rising up above the rest of the players to clear the ball.
Nearly missed it flying past him
as he misses it entirely.
Nearly missed the ball then land at the feet of the Meadowbank forward who can't believe his luck.
Nearly missed him scuff it over the line from three yards out. To equalise.

With six. Minutes. To go.

BASTARTS!!!!!

Song: Thirteen Seconds to Go

*

Narrator I get back on the bus the next day thinking about how monumentally I've fucked this.
I mean, even if they'd won I'd have still fucked it so why would I do such a stupid fuckin' . . . I'd fixed it, I'd pulled it back around. What the fuck was I thinking?

Head swirls, a memory.

Dad Sally, trust me, I know you don't want to come but you have to

Sally I don't have to!

Dad Look, it's hard, I know, unthinkably so, but I'll be there. And if you don't come, I think you'll regret it.
We can't change what happened.
But you can decide what you do here.
What's it to be Sally, eh?
Obviously it's up to you. I can't make you come.
But honestly, I think you'll regret it.
This is all bad enough without you having to live with that.

We are back in the present.

Aw maybe if I just get there and explain then . . . I might be able to . . . like if they'd just listen and understand, then maybe . . .

A beat.

Dad Sally, you know, there's difference between accepting defeat and accepting loss. And how as much as we might try /

Sally / Oh shut it, you!

Narrator Monday morning I stride in, prepared to fight for myself.

Sally Listen, I know that Saturday was an error but I can make up for it, I can . . .

Narrator . . . they're not listening.

Boss Sally, we thought you wanted this.

Sally I do, I just /

Boss / We really thought you were committed. To the team. What happened?

Sally I don't know, I just . . . I had to spread my dad's ashes and /

Boss / No, what happened to *you?* We really thought you would have what it takes.

Sally Aye, well it looks like we were both wrong.

Boss Sally, we're . . . perhaps not entirely convinced that you . . . belong here.

Sally Aye well, fair enough, I'm not really sure I belong anywhere.

Narrator So that's that then.

Song: What's Winning? *(Verse, Chorus, Bridge)*

A Low Ebb

Narrator So, on the 24th of January, my birthday, I tell my landlord I'm leaving and I pack up the flat. Well, if I'm going to be signing on, I may as well do it from Dad's.

I head north. My big world getting smaller and smaller as I do.
Well Dad, looks like you've won.

Song: What's Winning? *(Verse, Chorus, Bridge)*

Narrator I get into Edinburgh, pull a card out my wallet and head to Dunfermline.

Sally Hello, John McWhirter from the council,
I'd em . . . seeing as the three months aren't up yet, I was wondering if I could, em . . . yeah.

So, I get back to . . . *my* house in Cowdenbeath
and I feel
lost,
alone,

and
times like these I wish
I could
talk to my mum

but I can't

Instead I've got Margaret, offering me soup!

Oh would you just . . .!

Anyway let's erm . . . talk about the games shall we?

Of course they're still losing.
Because of course, they're still shite.

Narrator A 0-0 draw in the next round of the Scottish Cup against Premier League Hibernian has everyone's in bits; Bluebell the Cow's waving a Brazil flag while doing laps of the race track on a scooter, Auld One Syllable's greetin', big tough mining lads are greetin' with disbelief and joy at having nearly touched greatness.

I'm just greetin'!

*

Narrator And before the next game
I'm so desperate that I . . .

'Listen, eh . . . father? I don't normally do this kind of thing but, I don't even know if you're . . . look . . . is it me? Is there something I'm . . . not doin'? Just gonna . . . please, gonna help me?'

Beat.

Then Rod, Tod, Ned? says

Friend Oh aye, thought we were '*all equal in God's eye*'.

Sally Well, aye, but . . . I figured I could test that theory a little when it comes to Dunfermline!

Narrator (*to herself, to the fans, to the gods*)
Come on, give us something.
Can you no make them play like this is the Cup!
I mean this *is* a cup. If you think about it . . . The Pride Cup.
Imagine how good it would feel
if they could look at their oldest, smelliest rivals
and say:
'Ha! We beat you

and we're *SHITE!*
So how shite does that make you?! Eh . . . amen'.

Now COME ON!!!

The game starts, it finishes;
we're unsure how it's gone.

Look, right, I just want to say: I'm pretty liberal, right? And look, I know when people say that, it's often a precursor to you finding out, almost immediately, that they are very much not, in fact, a liberal.

But I am. Honestly. I've got compassion and understanding for everyone.
Right?
But see Dunfermline?
Absolutely fuck Dunfermline. Fuck the lot of them.

THE SCORE FLASHES UP – Cowdenbeath 1-2 Dunfermline.

Bastards.

And while we're at it – fuck this team.
Fuck this place.
Fuck the lot of it!

Song: One of these Days / Let's All Laugh About Them
(Reprise In Minor)

*

Narrator The next load of games blur into one big jumble for me here and if this was a sports movie, you'd probably get them all in some sort of montage right now of me doing things like: kicking sofas, pulling my hair and throwing Dad's stuff around the house, while scorelines flash up, thick and fast, one after the other.

February 17th: Cowdenbeath 1-1 Kilmarnock
February 23rd: Cowdenbeath 0-2 Dumbarton
February 27th: Cowdenbeath 0-2 Raith Rovers

But this is *not* a sports movie, so there is no montage. I am here
for every minute of every match and every minute of the days and weeks in between
as they play out in real time. Astonishingly agonising real time.

The montage of course would end with the back page of the paper spinning in to take up the whole screen with a story that tells us that defeat today at the hands of Stirling Albion would confirm the inevitable and see them become not just the first team in Britain to get relegated from any division this season but it would be the earliest point in any season that any team in Britain has ever been relegated from any division. There'd be a wee side article about all the other records they hold – like record number of fines for fielding illegible players, for example, *but there'll be nothing in that paper about me, what I'm going through, that I just need someone, to offer something that's going to help this team rise to the occasion and bring this all to an end.*
And if Dad hadn't been cremated in it, I'd stick his strip on and do better myself!

Song: Hooky and Jim *(Intro)*

Sally Go away Margaret!

Song: Hooky and Jim

*

Friend Come on then, let's find out if there's life in this manky old dog yet, shall we?

Narrator And well . . . they don't get relegated because they get . . . a draw!
And of course *everyone* . . . goes wild.
So do I.
Just in a very . . . different way.
Cause of all the places I *should* go in this moment, it's *not* Wee Jimmy's Bar. Where they're all celebrating staving off

relegation for a week like they'd just won the European Cup. Givin' it.

Friend Nah nah nah nah nah nah nah nah nah nah nah
we are stayin' up
Stayin' up
Weeee are stayin' uu-up!
nah nah nah nah nah nah nah nah nah nah nah

Sally Oh would you just stop it!

You realise it's actually statistically near impossible for them to actually stay up. Right?

Friend Well . . . aye, but we didn't go down today!

Sally Look, I don't even care if they relegated. I don't care if they fold and die, like they should have done years ago! I just need them to win one. Fucking. Home. Game. You do realise that, don't you? That we haven't won a game here all season?!

Narrator And he's like, *'oh. Is that true enough, aye?'*

Sally Well yes! Because otherwise, why the fuck else would I be here?
But what about you, eh? What the hell keeps bringing you back here to this drivel? At least I'm trapped here. What's your excuse?!

Narrator And I know that even though I'm shoutin' at *him* that really, I'm shoutin' at Dad.

Narrator I just, I thought that after enough games I'd see it. I thought I'd understand what it *was* about this place. What kept him here.

Sally He's right, it's an illness. It has to be! Why else would you stand through this when there is a whole world out there?!

I loved him. I loved him so fucking much. I wanted to be with him but not here,

Cause I couldn't be here. I couldn't, there was too much pain here.
I wanted him away from here. Away from the grey and the rain. Away from streets I couldn't walk down because it's where my mum was taken from me at twelve years old. Do you know what that's like, to come back to that?! I couldn't come back. He could have come to me. But he didn't! No one talks about that. Do they?! I was building something, something new, not stuck on history, and I'm the bad one? I'm the wanderer that never returns! I'm the heartless one that left him here?
I might have moved away. But he left me!

And then this?! This cruel game from beyond the grave?
A win?!

Seriously though. A win!
I get that he'd pick here.
But after a win?!
Did he have any idea what he was asking!?

Most people just pick a place they like. A place with significance, under a tree, up a hill, the Asda carpark they were conceived. But this is ridiculous.
It's just another layer of torture!
But that's the style, isn't it?!
Suffer and gloat. Suffer in the mines and romanticise it. Suffer on the terraces and call it the greatest team in the world. Suffer in this miserable grey town and call it home!
I'm done with it!
I'm done!
It ends here!

She raises the urn above her head
pauses for a moment
then throws it as far as she can.
Smash.

I'm going home.

All is Not Lost

Sally *is sat slumped at home looking though her dad's letters and articles.*

Narrator OK, so obviously this is a low.

I'm packing up. Even though I've got no idea where I'm gonna go.
When the door goes. Of course I shout

Sally Go away Margaret!

Narrator But I get back this meek wee
'Eh . . . it's no Margaret, its me'

Would it kill him to use his name just *once?!*

He says 'I'll just be a minute, I want to show me something'.

And he's stood there with this big daft look on his face, holding a supersize tub of funsize variety chocolate bars.

Sally What's this?

Friend 'Eh . . . it's your dad. Well, what's left eh him'.

Narrator Says he didn't want my last memory of this place to be throwing my dad's ashes across Wee Jimmie's dance floor in a rage.
Then he says:

Friend There's something else you need to know. Yer dad was sick. He'd been sick for a while.

Narrator And I'm like
'Aye, Mad Cowdenbeath Disease, contracted at birth'
but he says
'No, pneumoconiosis – black lung disease. He knew he was dying'.
And I'm like 'why didn't he tell me?'

Friend 'Well . . . cause he knew you'd come.
And that you'd probably eh *stayed*
and as much as he'd eh loved that,

he didnae want ye stuck here looking after him, he wanted you to live your life.
He'd be the same now.
He'd never eh asked for what he asked for if he'd known it would eh played out like this'

Narrator Then he tells me there was something Dad wanted much more than a win, a wish he never thought would come true;
To pass this club, its history, its values on to me.
In the hope that I would keep it alive so that his great-great-grandkids might still talk of the greats and dream of stepping into their boots one day.
He wanted for me not just to *know* it
but to have *lived* it.
To have suffered through it.
And well . . . I've certainly done that.

Friend 'You could scatter his ashes on the flyover of the Raith Interchange now and it wouldn't matter. He'd be happy.'

Sally . . . Aye.

A beat.

Narrator So we make a deal
that *whatever* happens, whether we win a game or not, we spread his ashes by the end of the season.

Friend You know what, I reckon he'd be alright with that.

And plus . . . *you never know?*

Final Four Games

Sally So, four more games. And it feels different.

OK, the first game's rotten and we're pumped 4-0 off of Hamilton but . . . we laugh about it.

Then they lose the next two matches by a respectable single goal each, both of them, heartbreakingly, coming two minutes from the final whistle. (Though, given that that those goals were the 100th and 101st we've conceded this season, I'm not sure if respect is a word we can really band around.)
But hey, some of the young lads are getting a game now and playing well, showing there are some green shoots for next season – that there might be a little blue in the sky.

And you know what, I can't believe I'm saying this, but I actually kind of enjoy it.

And it's not just the games I start to enjoy. I start going round with Auld One Syllable to some of the stuff around the games. Helping out with supporters groups that meet up during the week. Stuff he used to do with Dad. I thought it was all just auld boys meeting up to moan about the team and glorify the past. And well, aye, it kind of is that, but it's also a cup of tea, a bite to eat or just a conversation for anyone that might need it. It's . . . community. And I know this'll sound trite, twee even, but I see that supporter doesn't just mean 'being a fan' or turning up on a Saturday and demanding a win, it's supporting each other. I see it's no really about the football. No really. That's just the thing bringing them together, the thing that gives these tough buggers permission to be soft, kind and to look out for each other. To do good . . . here.

And get this, speaking of good. In the greatest, most glorious, most unsuspecting twist of fate, against all the odds, we beat . . . Dunfermline!
And we don't just beat them. We batter them . . . 2-0!
OK, it's away from home but Dad would have loved that so much more – to end this nightmare season by gubbing that lot on their own turf!
HA! WHO'S THE LAUGHING STOCK NOO, EH?
YAAAASSSSS!!!!

Big Craig, or Ross or Steve, tells me that the football world is so overawed by the sheer skill of the performance, that the Brazilian national team will, henceforth, be known as 'the Yellow Cowdenbeath'.
Although this rumour is, as yet, unconfirmed.

*

So, spirits are high going into the last home game.

And on that very morning, I get a letter offering me a job, in Glasgow, doing legal work for a charity that supports refugees and I could cry. And hey, I might not be one of the Chosen Few, but I feel lucky to be doing something that matters.
And even though I'm ready to move on, it suddenly hits me that this is probably the last time I'm gonna make this journey and . . .

I see the bag that Piff . . . Paff . . . Poff? brought round way back in August sitting, ignored, for nearly nine months.

I pull out his scarf and . . .

I can't believe it still smells fresh. Got it with his first pay packet when he was thirteen – all that time, all that coal, all that pie, all that Bovril. And it still smells fresh? Pride and joy.

That's a man that knew he belonged somewhere.

She puts it on.

Feels good.

Then I pull out his season ticket, the thickness of it, all those pages not torn out, pulls the last nine months into sharp focus, and when I pull it out the envelope, I see there's something else with it.

It's a clipping of a newspaper article he'd written after losing the last game of the season and missing out on promotion a few years ago.

She reads.

Dad Some thoughts on Cowdenbeath's defeat to Airdrie today.

Loss is hard, this team knows that all too well. So do the fans.
The town knows it too – having lived with the constant threat of a pit collapse, or explosion. And then there's the loss of the pits entirely and the loss of stability and livelihoods that went with them. There's countless losses that have broken the town's heart, left us all devastated. And that's on top of the everyday personal loss that all people, in all towns carry round with us – personal devastations that could break any of us. I know, mine nearly broke me.
But I'm grateful to say it didn't. How not? Well, if there's one thing I've learned about loss, it's that you can't hide from it, no matter how hard you try. You have to live with it, accept it as part of your life, or you'll be forever under its spell.

How do you do *that?* You might ask. How do *you* accept loss into your life? Well, like anything else, it takes practice.

And I've found there to be no better training ground for dealing with loss than at Central Park.

Watching this team lose more often than not, doesn't make me feel like a failure. It reminds me that, while times can be hard, and they often are, *greatness*, truly *great* moments are fleeting, and hard earned through struggle. And that's true of life. It reminds me that the counterpart of loss isn't victory, its hope. The hope that greatness, which has come before, *can* come again.

So, yeah, we lost today. And it hurts. But we know from experience it will pass.

And we fold it into the story.
Which, like the town's, is a story of people who know how to lose and keep going.

With hope over experience.
Because there is no other way.

And if you can do that, then eventually you'll come to realise that no loss ever needs to cost you your hope.

Song: What's Winning *(Reprise)*

Narrator I put the ticket in my pocket and I realise there's something I need to do before I go in.

Song: Come Home Now *(Verse and Chorus)*

Sally *rings a bell.*

Sally Margaret, I was wondering if you might want to walk me in to the game.

Narrator She says . . .

'Eh, No. You're alright. Thank you, Sally'.

And closes the door in my face!

A beat, surprised.

Narrator But she opens it a moment later, saying:

'I'm having you on pal, course I will, I'll away and get my coat'.

You see, I know why she's offered to walk me in all these times.
She's known I won't want to walk down that street. Where Mum was hit by a bus. And killed.
But I know I need to do it.
No more long way round. No more running.

We stop for a moment at the top of it.

Margaret Just take your time Sally. It'll be alright

. . .

Sally Will you tell me about her?

Margaret Of course I will.
She was mad.

In the best possible way. She was stubborn. Knew her mind. But she'd do anything for anyone. And never made you feel like you owed her. She was sweet. Wonderful. Strong. I loved her. We all did. And it would have broken her heart to not see you grown up. But I tell you, she'd be proud of you Sally.

Sally . . . OK . . . I'm ready

Narrator My feet wobble, my heart pounds, but . . .
It's just a road.
A horrible road. Where a horrible thing happened.
But it's part of the story and that has to be OK.
And so's Mum.
The name Jean McAlpine lives on.

Song: Come Home Now *(Verse and Chorus)*

Narrator I thank Margaret, I apologise (a lot!) and ask her if she'd like to join me for the game.

But she takes great pride in telling me that she
'*widnae watch that shite for aw the bridies in Forfar!*'

But says I can '*come by for a bowl eh soup later?*'

And eh . . . '*Aye. Aye, that would be lovely*'.

At the Stadium

Narrator I get to the stadium just in time for kick off but John . . . Don . . . Ron? isn't here yet. I can't do it without him. No way. He has to be here.

Then I notice Bluebell the Coo's wearing an oversized top with McAlpine on the back.
He wanders over and gives me a big hug.
And it's probably the best hug I've ever had.

Friend You ready Sally?

Sally I think I might be, aye.

Narrator Ok Dad, this is it.
Look at them battle. See their gargantuan effort; attacking and defending with their lives. And look – that young player bursting down the wing, stick thin and full of pace, Toothpick-esque wouldn't you say? And him – trapping the ball and flicking out to the opposite wing in one fell swooping movement like Hooky Leonard reborn. And that lad there, like a young Ally Venters, no? Can he spur them on to victory, scoring with mere moments to go, giving the other team no chance to reply.

Can you picture it? The players throwin' their shirts in the air to celebrate the final whistle and if you squint, just enough, you might even see the coal dust on their backs. Can you hear the roar of the crowd? Amplified by the thunderous chorus of thousands of workers who have appeared all around us. Euphoria takes over. A perfect, joyful ending.

But this is not a sports movie. And in reality it only takes Kilmarnock four minutes to score their first goal of what would be a 3-0 drubbing.

However . . .

Narrator Auld James, Jo, Rick? is absolutely delighted we lost!
And although I'd have put his teeth in for that a month ago . . . I kind of get it.
Sure, winning's great,
but *not* winning a single home game for a whole season? It's a better story. And after all, it's the stories that matter in the end, you know?

But then he says 'naw, that's no it!'
Right, so it turns out that before we beat Dunfermline (fuckin' yas by the way) they were sitting second in the league and an absolute shoo-in for promotion.
But . . . after we, and I'll say it again, beat them, they dropped to third, meaning they needed their promotion rivals to lose today if they were to have any chance of going

up. And who were their promotion rivals? That's right, Kilmarnock.

So, we cheer, we cry, we demand better next season, but most importantly – we celebrate playing a key role in Dunfermline's misery.
And even though I nearly put my back out, I even take a moment to enjoy a dangle on the hand rail. I'm happy.

OK. It's time. We head to the centre circle
and *everyone* has stayed to cheer us on as we do.
This crowd may be small. But it is mighty.

Sally *walks to the centre spot, takes a moment, before . . .*

Sally Well Dad, you missed a hell of a season.
We couldn't get you a win. But we made history.
Least amount of victories in a season.
Most losses in a season.
Lowest ever points tally in a season.
Lowest number of goals ever in a season
and the most goals ever conceded – 109!
Ya lucky bastard.
We are lucky, you and I.
Sure it'd be great if it'd all gone differently, won every game, brought in record crowds and topped the league. But hey, you can't change things. If we could, you'd not be in a tub, you'd be here beside me and so would Mum.

Plus, if we did win all our games, do you know how many games I'd have been at this season? One. So I'm glad they didn't.

And hey! We ruined Dunfermline's season
so maybe some things are more important than winning.

So many things are more important than winning.

Look, I'm sorry Dad.
I'm sorry I didn't go to Mum's funeral.
I'm sorry I couldn't see what you got from this,
couldn't see what were trying to show me by bringing me

here every week.
But I see it now.
So, thank you.
Thank you for trying.
And thank you for this season. OK, I thought at times I might never get through it.
But I feel I know much more about who you *were*, and much more about who I *am* as a result.
I love you Dad.
Goodbye.

She pours the ash.

Narrator I turn to Auld One Syllable and say

Sally Listen . . . mate, I don't think I ever thanked you for getting me through this.

Friend Aye well . . . thank *you*. I was dreading coming back without your dad but em . . . aye, so . . . Any time. I mean that.

Sally Absolutely. Well there is actually one thing I need to ask you.

OK, this is so embarrassing and please don't be offended but . . . what's your bloody name!?

Narrator And he says

Friend I tell you what. I'll tell you . . . the next time you're here at Central Park for a game. What do you say?

Sally I wouldnae miss it!

Song: Who Are the People

FULL TIME

www.ingramcontent.com/pod-product-compliance
Lightning Source LLC
LaVergne TN
LVHW052343100826
845147LV00021B/1165

* 9 7 8 1 3 5 0 6 6 3 7 4 9 *